GW00836339

Portsmouth

in old picture postcards

by
David Francis
and
Peter Rogers

European Library - Zaltbommel/Netherlands MCMLXXXV

GB   ISBN 90 288 3117 7 / CIP

European Library in Zaltbommel/Netherlands publishes among other things the following series:

IN OLD PICTURE POSTCARDS *is a series of books which sets out to show what a particular place looked like and what life was like in Victorian and Edwardian times. A book about virtually every town in the United Kingdom is to be published in this series. By the end of this year about 175 different volumes will have appeared. 1,250 books have already been published devoted to the Netherlands with the title* **In oude ansichten.** *In Germany, Austria and Switzerland 500, 60 and 15 books have been published as* **In alten Ansichten;** *in France by the name* **En cartes postales anciennes** *and in Belgium as* **En cartes postales anciennes** *and/or* **In oude prentkaarten** *150 respectively 400 volumes have been published.*

For further particulars about published or forthcoming books, apply to your bookseller or direct to the publisher.

This edition has been printed and bound by Grafisch Bedrijf De Steigerpoort in Zaltbommel/Netherlands.

INTRODUCTION

The Domesday Book mentions three manors on Portsea Island in 1086, namely Buckland, Copnor and Froddington (Fratton). Any associated habitation would have been very small, and the first substantial permanent settlement (in the south-west corner of the island) occurred in the last quarter of the twelfth century. The importance of the harbour was apparent from earliest times, but it was not until the early eighteenth century that development took place beyond what is now known as Old Portsmouth, on to Portsmouth Common. Portsea, as this new suburb came to be called officially in 1792, also grew rapidly and housing for workers in the ever expanding dockyard spread northwards and eastwards. Southsea had its beginnings in the early nineteenth century, first as an area where the better off could find more space than in the fortification-subscribed limits of Portsmouth and Portsea, and later as a sea-side resort. North End originally developed as a rural retreat for the more wealthy, but, by the early years of this century, most of Portsea Island was built on, apart from its northern and eastern extremities. The borough and latterly city boundaries extended at various times to meet this expansion until they took in parts of the mainland as well.

The bombs of the Second World War made the biggest changes in the appearance of Portsmouth. The demolition of the fortifications around 1870, some slum clearance in the 1930s, and post-war redevelopment and road construction have also contributed. This little book does not purport to tell the complete physical history of the city, but it is hoped that the detail in the text will make it more than simply an uncritical wallow in nostalgia.

The definitive history of Portsmouth has yet to be written, and none of the attempts at doing so at any length is now in print. The interested reader is referred to: B. Masters, The growth of Portsmouth, (3rd edition revised by N. Yates), Portsmouth City Records Office, 1979, which provides a brief, but well written and reliable, introduction.

Portsmouth City Council is a major publisher in local history. Its 'Portsmouth Records Series' is a major contribution to scholarship, consisting of documents and bibliographies edited to the highest academic standard. The inexpensive series of 'Portsmouth Papers' are well researched, well illustrated and well produced booklets on specific topics such as railways, theatres, public houses and churches, and also more discursive aspects of Portsmouth's history. It also keeps in print the 'Records of the Corporation' series, year by year accounts of the major civic events from 1835 until 1965, and from 1966 to 1974 on a thematic arrangement.

The complete bibliography of Portsmouth will number many hundreds of items, and the few listed below are simply those which have been drawn on most heavily in compiling this book. The work done by their authors is acknowledged with thanks.

A. Corney: *Fortifications in Old Portsmouth — a guide.* Portsmouth City Museums, 1965.

E. Course: *Portsmouth railways. (Portsmouth Papers no. 6).* Portsmouth City Council, 1969.

W. Curtis: *Southsea: its story.* Bay Tree Publishing Co., 1978.

S.E. Harrison: *The Tramways of Portsmouth.* Light Railway Transport League, revised edition, 1963.

M. Hoad: *The origins of Portsmouth. pp. 1-30 in 'Hampshire Studies',* Portsmouth City Records Office, 1981.

R. Hubbuck: *Portsea Island churches. (Portsmouth Papers no. 8).* Portsmouth City Council, revised edition, 1976.

R.C. Riley: *The growth of Southsea as a naval satellite and Victorian resort. (Portsmouth Papers no. 16).* Portsmouth City Council, 1972.

Mr. L. Bern must also be acknowledged for invaluable work on cinemas, road transport, and St. Mark's Church.

Our grateful thanks are also due to Mr. J. Thorn, Mr. A. King and the staff of the Portsmouth District Central Library and to Miss S. Peacock and the staff of the Portsmouth City Records Office for their unfailingly patient help and advice; thanks to them, too, for permission to reproduce copyright material; similarly to The News, Portsmouth, Messrs. Lens of Sutton, Portsmouth City Council, Portsmouth City Museums, Peter Relf, and Bill Buckley and Pru Read of Point Collectors' Centre, Broad Street; illustrations which are acknowledged to these individuals or bodies *remain their copyright;* thanks also to Mr. R. Allen, Mrs. P. Barker, Mr. D. Jordan, Mr. D. Naylor, Mrs. B. Reeves, Mr. G.J. Rogers, Mrs. F.M. Savage and Mr. M. Southcott for making material available, and to Roger Macdonald, Angela Mitton and Dr. James Thomas for various help and encouragement.

The two oldest parts of our city, Old Portsmouth and Portsea, are covered first in this book. Southsea and Landport/Fratton grew roughly in parallel during the nineteenth century and, arbitrarily, the former is treated next, with Milton and Copnor added. Landport and Fratton give way to North End and Hilsea as we move northwards up and off Portsea Island. After a few scenes of mainland Portsmouth in the past, we conclude with a look at some bygone forms of public transport.

28 PORTSMOUTH
The Parish Church. —

1. In spite of claims for Henry I and Richard I as founders of Portsmouth, the honour should really go to John de Gisors, who by the 1170s owned a lot of land on Portsea Island. Reputedly a Norman shipowner, he was attracted by the natural advantages of the Camber as a harbour and set about founding a borough in the area in or about 1180. He provided the land for a church, in an area known as Sudwede. The church, consecrated in 1185, was the first in England to be dedicated to St. Thomas à Beckett. It was a daughter church of St. Mary's, Portsea, until 1320, and served simply as a parish church until 1927, when it became the cathedral of the new Anglican diocese of Portsmouth. It has since been considerably enlarged.

PORTSMOUTH PARISH CHURCH—*View from N.W. of Nave.*

2. The original church had a low tower between the transepts. This and the nave were seriously damaged in the civil war. On 3rd September 1642, Roundhead forces in Gosport fired on the tower because it was being used as a look-out by the still royalist garrison. The church was repaired by 1693 with a new tower at the west end. This view shows some of the interior before the extensions of 1927-1939. The nave became the choir of the new cathedral. The gallery was built in 1708 and extended all round the transepts by 1750. It was reduced in size in 1904, and again, to its present position, in 1938.

3. This view of the oldest part of Portsmouth from around the turn of the century shows how crowded and cluttered it must have been, with barracks (visible bottom left) jostling with the premises of fishermen, stevedores and others who made their living from the sea, houses, pubs (there were nearly fifty in the eighteenth century), pawn-shops and numerous places of entertainment (to put it politely) for the soldiers and sailors who thronged the area. This district used to be known as Spice Island, apparently from the bad smell of the mud in the Camber at low tide — although other explanations have been suggested!

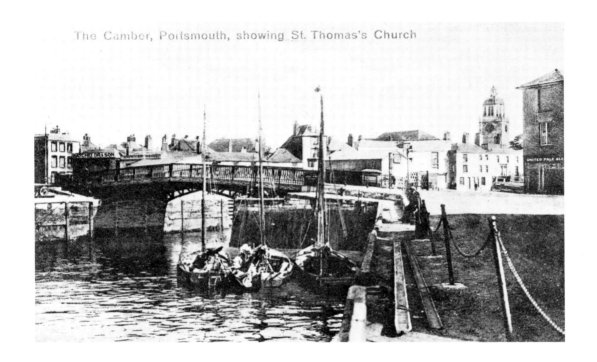

4. It was the Camber's potential as a haven that most attracted John de Gisors, and indeed Richard I when he gave Portsmouth its first charter in 1194. The first buildings were round its south and east sides. The Camber was formerly much wider than it is today, and there was a ford at low tide between Smock Alley, (now East Street), to the Town Quay on the other side. The Camber has long been a commercial port. In 1842-43, improvements were made; the inner Camber was deepened, and a swing bridge provided. There were more improvements in 1874, and the swing bridge was replaced by that illustrated in 1906. This lasted until 1927.

5. Portsmouth's ancient Camber docks in 1915 showed imagination and great enterprise when Messrs. Fraser and White installed massive handling and storage plant to facilitate the off-loading of seaborne coal. The storage structure of re-inforced concrete, involving many innovative building methods, was 240 feet long by 97 feet wide and could contain 15,000 tons of coal.

Garrison Church, Portsmouth.

6. The Garrison Church is a descendant of the chapel of the Domus Dei hospital founded about 1212 by Peter de Rupibus, Bishop of Winchester. The hospital was dedicated to Saint Nicholas, the chapel to Saint John the Baptist. As a monastery, it was dissolved in 1540, but as late as 1588 the hospital admitted seamen injured in the action against the Spanish Armada. It was subsequently extended into a house for the Governor of Portsmouth, and it was there (not, as is sometimes stated, in the church) that Charles II married Catherine of Braganza in 1662. In the 1860s the church was restored to serve the garrison, and many a spectacular parade took place. Bombed on 10th January 1941, it now stands roofless, an ancient monument.

ROYAL GARRISON CHURCH, PORTSMOUTH.

J. Russell & Sons, Royal Photographers, Southsea.

7. Many of the furnishings and fittings of the church were memorials. 23 memorial windows, the lectern, (a memorial to Queen Victoria), the pulpit and many benches in the nave were destroyed. Fortunately, memorial stalls to twelve chaplains who died in the Crimea campaign were saved. King George III presented a prayer book to the church in 1770, Queen Victoria gave six service books in 1875, and each succeeding monarch also donated books for devotional use. These were all removed for safe keeping at the outbreak of the war and so survived the blitz.

8. England's links with Normandy in the twelfth and thirteenth centuries optimised the advantages of the town as a port. This in turn made it an attractive point of attack from France in time of war and in 1338, 1369, 1377 and possibly 1380 the town was sacked. This led to it being fortified, increasingly extensively, so by 1687 it was surrounded by a complicated series of walls, moats, bastions and ramparts. The main entrance was the Landport Gate, serving the road to London. The gate shown here was built in 1760. It gave on to Warblington Street, not High Street, as the diverted road now does, perhaps to leave the town's principal road defensible even if the gate itself were taken. It is the only gate surviving in its original position.

9. King James' Gate stood across Broad Street, immediately beyond the junction with White Hart Road. It was built in 1687 as part of Sir Bernard de Gomme's extensive improvements at that time. This view is looking from Point. Point was thus outside the town walls, and consequently outside the town's jurisdiction after dark when the gates where shut, which did nothing to reduce its notorious reputation. There was also a moat outside the gate, running from the Camber to the sea. The gate was taken down sometime after 1874, but it still survives in attenuated form in Burnaby Road, serving as an entrance to the United Services Officers' playing fields.

"Old Portsmouth" Post Cards. Pub. by W. H. Barrell, Portsmouth

KING GEORGE'S GATE

10. Quay Gate breached the walls at the end of what was King Street and Crown Street, near the site of the present day roundabout between Lombard Street and Gunwharf Road. It gave access to the Town Quay and immediately faced the Camber bridge. The impressive gate illustrated was built in 1734, replacing an open arch in the wall a little to the north. It had a particularly large guard-house, and the various apartments above included the offices of the Governor in the eighteenth century. Quay Gate was demolished with most of the rest of the fortifications by 1871.

"Old Portsmouth" Post Cards, Pub. by W. H. Barrell, Portsmouth

KING WILLIAM GATE

11. King William's Gate was the fourth and last major gate of the town. It was built in 1833-34 to provide easy access to the developing resort of Southsea, replacing a small arch known as the Spur Gate. This provided so tortuous a path that it was known as the crooked arch. Its location was about half way along what is now Pembroke Road. The small gate on the left was for pedestrian use after the main gate had shut. The gate was gone by 1876, but its guard-house, now called The Cottage, still survives.

12. The bridge in the right foreground of the previous picture led on to King's Ravelin, a nearly triangular shaped bastion surrounded by the water of the moat. Another bridge, where the pair of gentlemen on the right of this view are standing, led from there across the glacis to Pier Road beyond. This view, taken about 1870 at the time of the demolition of the fortifications, gives some idea of how wide they were. The large building in the background started life as the Pier Hotel in 1865. It closed as such at the outbreak of the Second World War, and since served several functions before becoming a hall of residence to the Polytechnic in 1969. (Photo courtesy of Portsmouth City Museums.)

17 *PORTSMOUTH — General view of Barracks —*

13. Military use of the land made available by the demolition of the fortifications in the 1870s continued, and here we see the Victoria Barracks, begun in 1880. They stood on the site of today's Crest Hotel and part of Pembroke Park. Much of the building was done by convict labour, and W.G. Gates recounts a story of how the man responsible for some heraldic carvings on the outside of the barracks asked for an extension of his sentence so he could finish the job. Victoria Barracks, finally used as a training establishment for naval recruits, were closed in 1956, and the site was released by the Admiralty for development in 1962.

11 PORTSMOUTH. — *The George Hotel. In which Nelson spent his last Hours in England.* -

14. The George Hotel in High Street was at the time of its destruction in the blitz one of the most famous inns in Portsmouth. It had grown from humble beginnings in the early seventeenth century, when it was a small thatched affair called The Waggon and Lamb, into a most prestigious establishment by the end of the next. Midshipmen stayed at The Blue Posts in Broad Street, lieutenants in The Fountain, elsewhere in High Street, but only the most senior officers stayed at The George. Lord Nelson spent his last hours ashore in its room 15 on 14th September 1805, before leaving for his flagship H.M.S. Victory, and the Battle of Trafalgar.

15. Lord Nelson was idolised as a hero in his own life-time, and such a crowd had gathered at the front of The George on the morning of his departure that to avoid them, he slipped out of a rear window and through the back streets to gain the shore and H.M.S. Victory. Seen many years later, but still retaining an antique atmosphere, is the rear entrance of The George.

16. Some idea of the dignity of the old High Street is conveyed by this view from the south-west end. High Street was in the eighteenth and nineteenth centuries very much the social, commercial and recreational centre of the town. Some buildings that stood between the parish church and the street itself were demolished in the last decade of the nineteenth century, but otherwise Old Portsmouth really *was* old until the blitz wiped away most of it. The impressive building on the right, on the corner of Grand Parade, was at one time a bank, and a little further up, opposite Oyster Street, was The Fountain Inn, which in the mid-nineteenth century rivalled The George as the most prestigious in the town.

The Soldiers' Institute, Portsmouth.

17. The Fountain could reputedly accommodate 170 guests, and at one time had a resident laundress with several staff to cope with all their linen. But it declined, and by 1872, following a death at a boxing match held there, it was closed. Two years later it became the home of Sarah Robinson's Soldiers' Institute. This is a rear view, with some function going on in the garden. After Miss Robinson's retirement, it was run by the Y.M.C.A., and it was only demolished, after some controversy, in 1970.

18. Sarah Robinson (1834-1921) sought to spread Christian standards of morals and behaviour among soldiers. She began her work in Aldershot, visiting barracks and brothels, and encouraging temperance activities. She established a permanent Soldiers' Institute at the old Fountain Inn in 1874, where accommodation and other facilities were provided for soldiers, sailors and their wives. She extended her work to the needy of Portsmouth, providing a coffee house, laundry, and various night schools. Like Agnes Weston (see picture 120) she earned the opprobrium of those who made a living exploiting soldiers and sailors, but the great respect of the majority of her fellow citizens. Never enjoying robust health, she retired in 1899.

The Museum, Portsmouth.

19. This building was the third of Portsmouth's Town Halls. It stood in High Street, immediately to the south of The Dolphin Hotel. The first Town Hall was built in the 1530s, in the middle of High Street. This was replaced, on the same site, by 1739. The first floor of the new building, supported by Corinthian pillars, housed the council chamber and offices, and there was a market underneath. This hall became such an encumbrance to traffic that it was replaced by the building illustrated in 1838. When the present Guildhall opened in 1890, this became the town's museum, only to become a victim of Nazi bombs.

20. Here is St. Mary's, *Portsmouth*. Designed by Thomas Ellis Owen, it stood in St. Mary Street (later Highbury Street), serving as a chapel of ease to the parish church from 1839 to 1921, when, redundant, it was demolished. It stood about 100 yards on from where Highbury Street now ends, on a site subsequently engulfed by the recently (1984) demolished power station. It took its name from a mediaeval chapel dedicated to Our Lady of Closze, built circa 1320, which used to stand near the site. Some of this chapel's remains are said to have been used in rebuilding the parish church in 1692, and material from the church illustrated in the construction of the Trafalgar Cinema in Arundel Street in 1924.

21. John Pounds is one of Portsmouth's most worthy sons. Crippled by a fall in the dockyard in 1781, he became a shoemaker who, in the words of the inscription on his memorial in the garden of the Unitarian Chapel in High Street, 'while working at his trade in a very small room, gratuitously instructed in a useful education and partially clothed and fed some hundreds of boys and girls'. His work was a great example to the founders of the Ragged School movement. He died in 1839, but his house was preserved. As 78, Highbury Street, it was taken down at the outbreak of war in 1939. After the war, the timbers were found to be too rotten to re-erect, and, anyway, the power station was soon to extend over the site.

22. The Blue Posts, in Broad Street, was the third of the great inns of Old Portsmouth. It was there in 1613, and until the railway era was one of the principal coaching inns of the town. It was from the Blue Posts that one Andrew Nance, driving the coach Tantivi, set the record time to London of 5 hours 42 minutes. The Blue Posts was a well-known haunt of midshipmen, and it features in several of the novels of Captain Marryat. It was destroyed by a fire on 7th May 1870. This picture shows its replacement, named somewhat untruthfully The Old Blue Posts. This one was destroyed during the Second World War.

THE FLOATING BRIDGE,
PORTSMOUTH AND GOSPORT.

23. On 4th May 1840, the Port of Portsmouth Floating Bridge Company began operating the first regular ferry service across Portsmouth Harbour from Point to Gosport, using steam-powered chain ferries designed by J.M. Rendel, who invented the system a few years earlier. Departure from Gosport was on the hour and half hour, from Point on the intervening quarters. The first bridge could carry 20 carriages and 500 passengers. Although the service was sometimes erratic and the queues long, in the era of the horse such delays were preferable to the day's travel it took to reach Gosport by road. After the Second World War, a number of factors led to declining profitability for the company, and the final service ran on 15th December 1959.

24. To compete with the steam launches that replaced oar-powered wherries on the Portsea to Gosport crossing about 1869, the Floating Bridge Company introduced a service of launches of its own from Point. They were faster and more frequent for pedestrians than the half-hourly schedule provided by the floating bridges, and the service lasted until a bomb in the war destroyed their pontoon. However, the company was listed in local directories as The Port of Portsmouth Floating Bridge and Steam Launch Company until its demise. This view also provides a look at The Star and Garter (on the left at the end of Broad Street), another of Portsmouth's famous old inns. (Photo courtesy of The News, Portsmouth.)

25. The Star and Garter dated from the mid-sixteenth century. It was one of Portsmouth's more 'up-market' inns, and many famous admirals, including Nelson, Howe and St. Vincent, as well as the exiled French King Louis Philippe, and the authors Dickens and Thackeray are known to have stayed there. The Star and Garter survived the war, but was sacrificed not many years afterwards to provide new berthing facilities for the Isle of Wight car ferries. Here we see a car ferry at its original terminal at the end of Broad Street in the 1930s, with The Star and Garter on the right.

Portsmouth Shipping Cattle

26. Motor vessels had begun work on the Portsmouth-Isle of Wight ferry service in 1927, with the introduction of the M.V. Fishbourne, and a little later by M.V.s Wootton and Hilsea. Prior to that date animals and vehicles were conveyed in barges, known as tow boats or horse boats, hauled by tugs. There were five of these, ranging in length from 45 to 50 feet, in beam 16 to 17 feet, and in weight 17 to 22 tons gross. Fully laden they required only two feet of water. Three survived until the arrival of the motor vessels.

OLD PORTSMOUTH (POINT) A VIEW FROM BROAD STREET LOOKING TOWARDS HARBOUR AND DOCKYARD

27. Our last look at Broad Street shows a queue of vehicles for the Floating Bridge. Such traffic always queued on the left, the Isle of Wight traffic on the right.

SALLY PORT, OLD PORTSMOUTH.

28. This view of the west side of Point from the sea is encapsulated in its period by the piece of military impedimenta in the centre. This is a First World War search-light emplacement which, like a lot of other modern military hardware that has cluttered up the Portsmouth scene from time to time, had a fortunately short existence. There were similar emplacements at various other points along the sea-front.

29. Permission to build what was to be called King William Pier was got from the Admiralty in 1836, but as it was not ready until 1842, it had to be called Victoria Pier instead. Even so, it was still the first public pier in Portsmouth, and was very popular in its early days. In 1854 it was recorded that 'there were few piers in England, irrespective of those on the Thames, at which so many steamers called, as at the Victoria'. A dividend of 100% was paid to shareholders in 1860! But with the opening of the piers in Southsea, its popularity declined and it was not greatly mourned when it was destroyed in a storm in 1925. The existing Victoria Pier was built by the Corporation in the early 1930s.

Queen Street.

Portsea.

30. By the early eighteenth century there was no longer room in Old Portsmouth for houses for the increasing number of dockyard workers, and buildings started appearing on Portsmouth Common. This provoked opposition from the military Governor of Portsmouth, and it was only after a petition to Queen Anne via her husband Prince George that development was officially permitted. Queen Street, in the early days the fashionable shopping street of the 'new town' of Portsea, and the parallel Prince George Street commemorated this royal assistance. Queen Street soon ceased to be fashionable, and with its neighbourhood acquired a reputation which might be euphemistically described as 'lively'.

"Old Portsmouth" Post Cards. Pub. by W. H. Barrell, Portsmouth

LION GATE

31. The 'new town' of Portsea was fortified as extensively as Portsmouth, as late as the 1770s. It was thus almost certainly the last town in the world to be given city walls on what was really a mediaeval concept. Two gates were provided. Lion Gate, shown here, was the principal entrance. It stood where what is now Edinburgh Road (then Lion Gate Road), joins Queen Street. After the demolition of the fortifications Lion Gate was moved in 1871 to serve as an entrance gate to Anglesey Barracks. In 1929, it was moved again and incorporated into the Semaphore Tower in the dockyard. (What was known for centuries as the dockyard is now officially the Naval Base; the latter term is used when referring to the current situation, the former with events and fixtures before the name changed.)

" Old Portsmouth " Post Cards. Pub. by W. H. Barrell, Portsmouth

UNICORN GATE

32. The other gate, Unicorn, was erected in 1778-79, about a year after Lion Gate. It stood near the top of York Place. It survived there until 1873, when it was taken down and re-erected some 400 yards to the east, where it still serves as an entrance to the Naval Base, somewhat taller and thinner than in its original form shown here. There was a third gate in Portsea for about twenty years from about 1845 called Anchor Gate. This was provided to give the citizens a new means of access to the waterside after dockyard extensions blocked their route, and still survives in name in the Naval Base.

33. Orange Street ran parallel to and two blocks north of the now much redeveloped Cumberland Street. The name commemorated the Royal House of Orange, and names of other streets in the area reflected eighteenth century personalities and events: Marlborough Row, the famous Duke; Hanover Street, another royal house; Union Street, the union of England and Scotland; and so on. Orange Street was the location of the first Congregationalist Chapel in Portsea, opened in 1754. Orange Street disappeared about 1936, as part of a five-year slum clearance scheme initiated by the Council in 1933. (Photo courtesy of Point Collectors' Centre.)

34. Blossom Alley ran parallel to Prince George Street, connecting Cross Street with North Street, an area where, as other writers have remarked, the blossoms were often faded! On the morning of Saturday 23rd January 1923, Blossom Alley achieved specific notoriety with the discovery of the murder of Mary Pelham in number 14. Mary was a prostitute, but she had a good deal of local popularity for many acts of kindness and helpfulness as well. The murderer was never found, nor was a definite motive established, but the case did at least force to public attention the squalid state of the slums of Portsea, and a few years later many of them were cleared, often by the simple expedient of burning. (Photo courtesy of Point Collectors' Centre.)

35. St. George's Square took its name from the church built at the instigation of local people in 1753-54, and the area remained fashionable for longer than the rest of Portsea. John Wesley's first visit to Portsmouth in 1753 found him preaching here. In Britain Street, just to the east, Isambard Kingdom Brunel of ship, bridge and railway fame, was born in 1806. A pleasant description of the church and its congregation in the nineteenth century appears in Sir Walter Besant's novel 'By Celia's Arbour', where it is disguised as St. Faith's. Dilapidation, Hitler's bombers and redevelopment have wrought many changes in this area over the years, but fortunately the church is still standing and active.

36. St. John's Church in Prince George Street was second only to St. George's in Portsea, being opened by the Bishop of Winchester on 31st July 1789. It was a proprietary chapel and until 1835 had no parish, but derived its income entirely from pew rents. Its ministers were always ardently evangelical, an interesting contrast with Holy Trinity, a short distance away in North Street. Reverend Lindsay Young, incumbent from 1881 to 1933, was one of Portsea's best known characters. St. John's was destroyed in an air raid on 12th August 1940. Coincidentally, there was also a Roman Catholic chapel dedicated to St. John in Prince George Street in the nineteenth century. (Photo courtesy of The News, Portsmouth.)

37. Above: Holy Trinity, at the end of North Street, was the third Anglican church to be built in Portsea. The foundation stone was laid on 20th June 1839, but damage by local hooligans delayed its consecration until 30th September 1841, the same day as St. James', Milton. With the arrival of Thomas Platt as vicar in 1854, it became the first Anglo-Catholic church in Portsmouth, and for a time attracted a lot of attention. Restoration and improvement work took place in 1877, but by 1906, Holy Trinity was surplus to requirements and was sold to the Admiralty for £5,000, to serve as a chapel to the Naval Barracks. (Photo courtesy of Portsmouth City Council.)

Right: The dockyard walls were extended round the church in 1907, and it served its new purpose peacefully until wrecked by bombs in 1941. It was finally deconsecrated on 21st April 1948. One wall still survives, and the vicarage is still used as a residence for a naval official. The statuettes behind the altar pictured here were carved by shipwrights among the congregation and presented as part of the improvements of 1877.

Mudlarks

89545

38. The viaduct to the Harbour Station and Gosport Ferry pontoon replaced the not very successful Royal Albert Pier (opened in 1847) in 1876, when the railway was extended thus far from its previous terminus at the Town Station. Mudlarks, begging for pennies, shocked or entertained thousands, especially the queues for the Isle of Wight ferries on summer Saturdays. They were descendants of the 'Common Hard Kingers', lawless rascals who had a headquarters called the North Pole among the darker recesses under the Harbour Station. The viaduct was rebuilt on a new alignment in 1968, and this finally put an end to mudlarking.

THE HARD
PORTSMOUTH

39. The Common Hard is technically the strip of made up area that leads into the water at right angles to the road shown here, but it is the road itself, with the gate into the Naval Base at the end that is known to most people as 'The Hard'. The area used to be known as 'The Devil's Acre' from the large number of pubs and brothels it accommodated. A good number of at least the former are seen in this view, which is also interesting for the variety of motive power in public transport vehicles it shows: electric trams, petrol driven taxis, and horse-drawn cabs. The Hard survived the war reasonably well, but there is no longer the wide variety of brewers' names adorning the still several pubs.

40. Ferries from Portsmouth to Gosport have existed for centuries. Steam launches appeared in 1869, and operated the services until 1966, when the existing vessels came into use. (Diesel power had been tried in latter years.) The railway viaduct led to the South Railway Jetty in the dockyard. It was used for troop trains and occasional specials for visiting dignitaries arriving at or departing from Portsmouth. Its last Royal use was in 1937 for the Coronation Review of the Fleet, and it was finally demolished in November 1960.

H.R.H. PRINCE OF WALES INSPECT CADETS. BEFORE EMBARKING ON THE "INDOMITABLE"

CRIBB. 2.

41. Here we see the then Prince of Wales (later King George V) on the South Railway Jetty on 15th July 1908. He was inspecting a guard of honour of cadets, prior to embarking on H.M.S. Indomitable for a visit to Quebec, where he inaugurated the Plains of Abraham as a National Park. The Prince was an enthusiastic sailor, and, buoyed up by the success of the visit, he is said to have helped stoke the boilers of the spanking new cruiser on the return journey.

H.M.S. VICTORY, PORTSMOUTH

42. H.M.S. Victory is one of Portsmouth's principal attractions. A first rate ship of the line, she was launched at Chatham in 1765, and served as flagship variously to Admirals Keppel, Hardy, Geary, Hyde Parker, Kempenfelt, Howe, Hood and St. Vincent. She was recommissioned in 1803 as flagship to England's greatest naval hero, Admiral Lord Nelson. After the Battle of Trafalgar in 1805, she served mainly in the Baltic. In 1840, Victory was moored in the harbour, where she remained until 1922, when she was moved into the dry dock in Portsmouth dockyard which has become her permanent home. Between 1922 and 1928, she was restored to her 1805 appearance, which explains the difference between the way she looks in this view from the way she looks now.

43. The practice of accommodating convicts, usually those awaiting transportation, in old ships known as prison hulks was established in the eighteenth century. It was during the period 1803-1814, when 14 such hulks in Portsmouth and Langstone harbours housed nearly 10,000 French prisoners of war that they attracted a lot of attention locally. Conditions aboard were vividly described in Louis Garneray's 'The French Prisoner' (Merlin Press 1957). The Portsmouth hulks continued in civilian use after the French wars until the construction of a new prison in Portsea in 1853, when the only use for them was as infirmary ships.

44. To most Portmuthians, H.M.S. Vernon is the establishment in St. George's Road dealing with torpedoes and mines. This has been the case since the end of the First World War. Before then, H.M.S. Vernon was a frigate. In 1872, she was moored in Fountain Lake next to H.M.S. Excellent (which housed the Navy's gunnery school), to serve as a torpedo instructional vessel. H.M.S. Excellent became land-based on Whale Island in 1891, but it was not until 1919 that the land at the old Gunwharf was acquired from the Army for the torpedo and mining school, and the old floating H.M.S. Vernon scrapped.

Kings Terrace, Southsea.

45. Southsea started life, like Portsea, as an overspill area from Portsmouth. A few artisan dwellings appeared in the Hambrook Row area in the first years of the nineteenth century on land owned by one Thomas Croxton, whence the name Croxton Town. Southsea as a residential area for wealthier people started with the Terraces. Landport, Jubilee and Bellevue Terraces were complete by 1815 and Hampshire Terrace and the most prestigious, King's Terrace, were by then under construction. Here is King's Terrace, before its destruction in the blitz.

Government House, Portsmouth.

46. After the demolition of the fortifications in the 1870s, the Services made alternative use of the land, and what is now the Polytechnic's Ravelin Park, in the triangle of Hampshire Terrace/Museum Road/Cambridge Road, became the centre of the garrison establishment. This building is Government House, which replaced a similarly named establishment in High Street in 1882. It stood where a Donkey Lane used to pass across the site, very close to where the Polytechnic's Frewen Library now stands. Government House was destroyed by an incendiary bomb in October 1940.

47. A dispensary for treating patients with eye and ear disorders had a short-lived existence in St. George's Square from 1821. The establishment which eventually moved into the ophthalmic unit at Queen Alexandra Hospital in 1970 began in 1884 in the premises shown here, on the corner of Pembroke Road and Clarence View. The hospital expanded rapidly and these buildings had been demolished and replaced by 1898. Bomb damage in January 1941 caused the hospital to use temporary accommodation in Kent Road and then at Liss before moving into the former Convent of the Holy Cross in Grove Road North in 1944.

48. In the late eighteenth and early nineteenth century, there was a considerable increase in the number of non-conformist places of worship in Portsmouth. This provoked a reaction within the Church of England and, with the aid of grants from a parliamentary commission set up to provide new churches in areas of rapid urban growth, All Saints and St. Paul's (illustrated here) Churches were built. Francis Goodwin, who subsequently designed several churches in various parts of the country, was the architect. St. Paul's faithfully served its district from its consecration in October 1822 until March 1941, when it was bombed and burnt out. The shell survived until 1958, when it was finally demolished.

49. There were efforts to establish Southsea as a watering place in the first decades of the nineteenth century. By 1825, a Mr. Hollingsworth developed a modest pump room into the large assembly room and baths shown here. They were named after the Duke of Clarence and changed when he became King William IV, to King's Rooms. The buildings were made of wood to facilitate demolition if ever neighbouring shore batteries needed to fire across the site. A quarrel at a ball here in 1845 led to the last fatal duel in this country, between Lieutenant Hawkey of the Royal Marines and Captain Seton of the 11th Dragoons. This view also shows Clarence Pier as originally built.

SOUTHSEA BEACH

50. The next development of Southsea as a resort was the construction of Clarence Esplanade, from King's Rooms to Southsea Castle, in 1848. It replaced a more rudimentary promenade made in 1807. Lord Frederick Fitzclarence, the Lieutenant-Governor of the town, and son of the aforementioned Duke, was influential in its construction, which was done largely by convict labour. This part of Southsea has always been particularly bustling, with vending stalls, boat trips, and in earlier days bathing machines.

51. Here is a view of the Esplanade looking west, towards Clarence Pier and the old King's Rooms, which in 1877 became the Esplanade Hotel. The Esplanade has attracted a variety of monuments to various naval heroes. A more grizzly sight on the beach here until about 1782 was the gibbet where the remains of John Felton, the murderer of the Duke of Buckingham in 1628, are said to have hung.

SOUTHSEA. CLARENCE PIER AND ESPLANADE.

52. Clarence Pier was built in 1861 by the Southsea Clarence Esplanade Company, the owners of the King's Rooms. In its original form it was a simple structure some 80 yards long with landing stages for Isle of Wight and other steamers (see picture 49). In 1865, the Landport and Southsea Tramway was built to provide a connection between the Town Station and the ferries. This was the first tram route in Portsmouth, and the first anywhere to have been set up by statute. The tracks originally ran right on to the pier, and this arrangement lasted until the main-line railway was extended to the Harbour Station in 1876. The large pavilion was added in 1882. It featured 'high class concert parties' during the week and 'sacred instrumental music' on Sundays, to quote an old guide book.

Clarence Pier from the Sea, Southsea.

53. Few boats now call at Clarence Pier, but in its hey-day one could go for excursions to various places along the coast, and on the Isle of Wight. This is how passengers on a departing boat saw the pier in pre-war days.

54. In early days, simply to provide some of the pleasures of being at sea without the associated discomforts was attraction enough for sea-side piers. This view captures the era when simply strolling on the pier (in one's best clothes, it should be noted), was a pleasure in itself — a great contrast with the bingo halls, fruit machines, electronic games and their accompanying din which are a *sine qua non* today.

Southsea Beach in the Season

55. Sea bathing existed in Portsmouth as early as 1754 at what is now Quebec House in Bath Square. There were some rudimentary bathing machines, and some huts known as MacDonald's Bathing Establishment at Southsea early in the nineteenth century, and the Board of Ordnance gave permission for the construction of more substantial accommodation near what is now Clarence Pier in 1816. This developed into the King's Rooms (see picture 49). The Portsmouth Swimming Club, whose bathing stages are shown here, began functioning in 1875. Visitors to the town could be accommodated for a small fee. The Corporation provided free shelters on various parts of the beach.

Portsmouth Swimming Club

56. The club's premises were a little to the east of the King's Rooms. Here is the imposing façade in the early years of this century. Such architectural opulence was perhaps justified for an organisation which, according to a 1911 guide book, had 1,500 members and was hence the largest society of its kind in the world.

Kings Road, Southsea

57. King's Road (originally Wish Street) completely changed character as a result of the blitz. Before the war, it was a fine shopping centre; indeed, it was Southsea's first, having twenty shops by 1830, and for many years it outshone Palmerston Road. In Hide's drapery, nos. 9-13, on the west corner of the junction with what is now St. Paul's Road (at that time Grigg Street), a young H.G. Wells served an unhappy apprenticeship in 1882; this no doubt provided some ideas for his novel 'Kipps'. King's Road was more or less flattened by bombs on the night of 10th-11th January 1941. It is considerably wider now than when it was photographed here.

46 SOUTHSEA. — *Kings Road and Elm Grove.* — ...

58. Here is Elm Grove, near its junction with what is now Castle Road on the right and Green Road on the left. (Originally Park Lane and Green Lane respectively, their junction is now somewhat re-aligned.) In, 1, Bush Villas, between the Bush Hotel and the church, a not overworked Doctor Conan Doyle turned to authorship, and it was here that the first Sherlock Holmes story was written, 'A Study in Scarlet' being published in 1887. Conan Doyle practised in Southsea from 1882 to 1890. His house, the church and the hotel were all destroyed in the blitz. A plaque on the side of the block of flats now on the site commemorates the 'birthplace' of the great detective.

59. Elm Grove Baptist Church was destroyed in the same air raid that accounted for Conan Doyle's house, next door. The building seen here was opened in 1881, the congregation having moved from their previous premises in St. Paul's Square a few years before. It cost over £9,000 to build and had seats for 1,000 people. The original congregation had broken away from the Kent Street Chapel about 1853.

Elm Grove, Southsea.

768.

60. Elm Grove was originally known as Wish Lane. Initially a road of residential villas, it was gradually turned into a shopping centre with the erection of one-storey extensions to their road frontages to make shops. Most of the elms which gave it its name had been sacrificed for this purpose by the end of 1902. In this view, taken around 1918, we are looking westwards towards the junction with Grove Road; what is now Telephone House has a car showroom on its site.

61. Elm Grove was well into its transformation from a residential to a commercial road when the Scala Picture House, the building on the right with the impressive classical arches, reputedly of granite, opened in 1917. It was on the south side, just west of Yarborough Road. The Scala was one of Portsmouth's smaller cinemas, seating 690 on opening, but also one of its best appointed. One account suggests it had a tea garden on the roof, or at least provision for one. The Scala was yet another of Portsmouth's buildings to be destroyed in the blitz of 10th-11th January 1941.

62. The Palmerston Road area of Southsea owes its development to the activities of Thomas Ellis Owen, architect and property speculator. Owen built numerous houses, villas and terraces from the 1830s until his death in 1862. Palmerston Road grew as a shopping centre to serve the fashionable populace who moved into Owen's desirable residences, and King's Road was ousted as the principal shopping area of Southsea. The Post Office was originally in this southern part of Palmerston Road, an area known as 'The Village' long after it was engulfed in a great city.

63. The northern part of Palmerston Road was already built up in Owen's time, although Owen himself designed and financed, at a cost of some £5,000, St. Jude's Church in 1851. The east side was known as Beresford Terrace, and the west side as Cambridge Terrace, although these were just of smallish houses. At the time of this picture, some fifty years later, Palmerston Road was already a long-established shopping street. Apart from those in the left foreground, every building seen here was destroyed in the blitz.

THE MIKADO CAFÉ, SOUTHSEA.

LARGEST CAFÉ ON THE SOUTH COAST.

VIEW OF THE GROUND FLOOR.

:: ::

64. Here is a scene of pure nostalgia. The Mikado Café stood on the east side of Palmerston Road, about halfway between Marmion Road and Stanley Street, in an area almost totally obliterated by the blitz. It claimed to be the largest on the South Coast. Live music in the palm court tradition was played all day, with the basket chairs and potted palms an essential part of the total environment.

65. Thomas Ellis Owen's father Jacob was himself an architect, and joined with Thomas in some of his ventures. They were responsible for the development of nearly all of Grove Road South, mostly in the 1840s. Here we are looking southwards, with St. Jude's Church in the distance. Grove Road had been a country lane before the Owens' operations; they turned it into a road of middle-class villas, still with a quiet, rural air. Today it is a busy, urban thoroughfare, with many commercial establishments, and a large school.

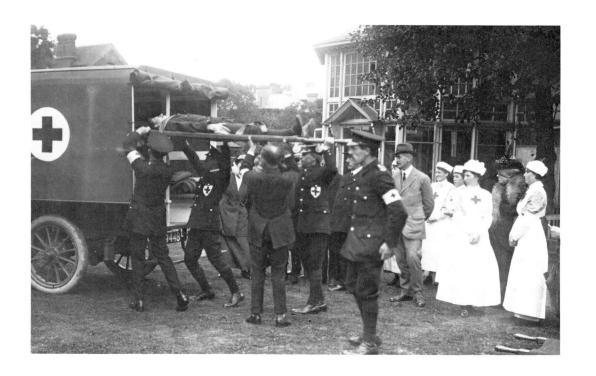

66. Brankesmere was a large house on the corner of Kent Road and Queen's Crescent, built in 1895 for the Brickwood family (the brewery magnates), on land made available by the demolition of two of Owen's houses. Its name changed to Byculla when a girls' school from Merton Road moved there about 1923. The school moved to Liphook at the outbreak of the war in 1939. Byculla eventually became the police headquarters and now, renamed Brankesmere, houses offices for the Social Services Department. In the First World War, Brankesmere was made available to the Red Cross as a relief hospital, and an episode from this phase in its history, perhaps a fête or open day, is illustrated here.

67. In keeping with its former status as a genteel resort, Southsea had a large number of independent schools between the wars. Byculla was a typical upper middle-class establishment aiming itself at the daughters of officers and gentlemen. Here is a scene at Speech Day 1926, with girls and parents segregated in suitable formality...

"BYCULLA". SOUTHSEA.   STEPHEN CRIBB. S'SEA

68. ...and here is a typical dormitory of the period, with suitably spartan facilities.

69. Handley's corner was one of the landmarks of pre-war Southsea. As an old guide book put it, it was 'a popular and fashionable parade ground with a constant stream of the élite of Southsea, and the walk of cultivated society'. When George Handley opened his shop in 1867, it was a single unit drapers. The business gradually expanded into neighbouring premises to become the best known store in Southsea. The name of the business survived for over a hundred years, before it was swallowed up by a national chain about 1973.

70. The Queen's Hotel was one of the earliest in Southsea. It was a conversion and enlargement of Southsea House, the home of Sir John Morris. The architect for the work was Augustus Livesay, who had designed both Holy Trinity and the first St. James' churches. The hotel opened in 1861, with its main entrance in Osborne Road. On 8th December 1901, in the first of a series of nine serious fires in Portsmouth in a fortnight, The Queen's Hotel was destroyed, with the death of two chambermaids. The present Queen's Hotel, to the design of T.W. Cutler, opened in 1903.

71. The first South Parade Pier was a private venture. It was opened on 26th July 1879 by Princess Edward of Saxe-Weimar, the wife of the Lieutenant-Governor of Portsmouth. (Waverley Road was called Saxe-Weimar Road until the First World War.) Concerts of music on the pier on Sundays caused some eyebrows to be raised among the more prudish inhabitants. The proprietors were energetic in their assertions that their pier was fire-proof, but these claims were ill-founded, for, on the afternoon of 19th July 1904, the first South Parade Pier was destroyed by fire. Fortunately, there were no casualties.

South Parade Pier, Southsea

72. Two years later, the Corporation purchased and demolished the derelict pier. It was replaced by this much more grand affair in 1908, representing an investment of £70,000. On completion, 800 men were hired for a day to jump up and down on the deck to test its stability. The main buildings housed a theatre and tea-rooms, while the seaward end was given over to roller skating round the bandstand, fishermen, and the many pleasure boats that called. Fortes leased the pier in 1967. There had been a number of minor fires over the years, but on 11th June 1974, while Ken Russell was using parts of the pier in making his film 'Tommy', there was a serious fire that destroyed most of the superstructure. The present superstructure was soon provided.

The Pavilion, South Parade Pier, Southsea

73. The pier's theatre was a gem of Edwardiana, full of plush and gilt. Almost every type of entertainment from straight plays to children's puppet shows was put on, and big name stars were always engaged for the summer season. Good quality amateur performances were also welcomed prior to 1967, and when the Southsea Shakespeare Actors staged 'Cymbeline' there in October 1966, they achieved the unique distinction of being the only entirely amateur company under an amateur director ever to have performed every one of Shakespeare's plays.

CANOE LAKE AND
SOUTH PARADE PIER, SOUTHSEA.

74. Prior to the nineteenth century, much of Southsea Common was a boggy wasteland, known as the Great Morass. The area around Craneswater, reputedly so called because it was the haunt of wildfowl, was a particular eyesore, being used as an unofficial rubbish dump. In 1884, the Corporation, now leasing the land from the War Department, improved matters by constructing the Canoe Lake. The borough engineer, H. Boulnois, recalls local opposition, one ex-Royal Engineers General complaining that he didn't want the sea any nearer his house, and the original plans were somewhat curtailed. However, when it was finished, in June 1886, the same ex-General was among the first to congratulate him on his successful transformation.

75. St. Bartholomew's Church in Outram Road had a complicated history. Consecrated on 1st December 1864, it acquired a district the following year. A mission church in the parish, St. Matthew's, opened in 1889, and this achieved parochial status in 1904. St. Matthew's was badly damaged by a bomb on the night of 10th-11th January 1941, so the two parishes re-united. However, St. Bartholomew's was in such a bad state of repair that restoring St. Matthew's was the cheaper alternative. In 1958, the rebuilt church was dedicated to the Holy Spirit, and, after a final service on 25th January 1958, St. Bartholomew's was closed and demolished. A small housing development on its site called St. Bartholomew's Gardens perpetuates its memory.

CRINOLINE CHURCH, EASTNEY.

Gain's Copyright.

76. This curious edifice is the *original* St. Bartholomew's Church, a very early example of a re-locatable building. Made entirely of wood, the twenty-sided structure was erected in 28 days, and opened on 24th October 1858, with a full congregation of some 520 people. It stood 58 feet high and was 72 feet in diameter. When the (still unconsecrated) new St. Bartholomew's was ready in 1862, the Crinoline Church, as it became nicknamed, was taken down and re-erected, again in 28 days, as a temporary St. Simon's Church in Waverley Road. Another four years on, it was removed to the Royal Marines Artillery Barracks in Eastney, where it is seen here, again serving as a temporary church until their St. Andrew's was built in 1905, when it was demolished.

Are You Coming Too.

Southsea Rly.

77. Southsea was at first a 'genteel' resort, a haven for retired persons and half-pay officers. However, by the 1920s, vigorous efforts were being made to promote Southsea and improve its facilities. A Beach and Publicity Committee was established, and in the years leading up to the war various attractions and amusements were provided. Here is an early view of the Southsea Miniature Railway still very much in the steam era, as on the main lines. Internal combustion engines eventually replaced the steamers, but in 1984 the railway was once more steam-operated.

Ladies' Mile, Southsea

78. A major boost to Southsea's appeal in 1923 was the purchase from the War Department of, and subsequent improvements to, Southsea Common. (Previously it had been simply rented.) The tree-lined section in front of Western Parade had for many years been known as the 'Ladies' Mile', a place for the fashionable to see and be seen, especially on fine Sunday mornings. Its length may be less than the statutory 1,760 yards, but the profusion of pretty young ladies to be seen there was sufficient for a writer in a 1937 guide book to aptly restate that 'a miss is as good as a mile'.

79. Victoria Road Methodist Church stood at the junction with Hamilton Road, where the housing development called Admiral's Corner now is. It was built in 1878 at a cost of some £8,000. Although it had strong links with the Daniel Street Chapel (it received financial aid from that source in 1882), it was officially an off-shoot of the Pembroke Road Church, until it became head of a new Southsea circuit in 1883. The church survived the blitz, but finally succumbed to declining congregations in 1971, when it was closed and subsequently demolished.

80. A long since vanished light industry of Portsmouth is brick-making on site. Portsea Island abounds in clay, and it was often scraped up from near the surface and put straight into clamps. Seen here in the early years of this century are workers on the site of Essex Road, which is listed for the first time in the 1904-05 Kelly's Directory. The White House public house is just visible in the background. All the men pictured are believed to be members of the Allen family, and their descendants still live in the area today. (Photo courtesy of Mr. R. Allen.)

VICTORIA HALL, SOUTHSEA'S CINEMA SUPERB.

81. In 1885 a group of local liberals erected the Gladstone Buildings. They subsequently became the Victoria Hall, which was used mainly as a ballroom. In July 1896 a moving picture show was staged. This was only a matter of months after the Lumières' first public performance in Paris, so certainly one of the earliest in this country. The 'Vic' became a full-time cinema in 1908, and in its early days was a luxurious establishment. Its glories had faded somewhat when it bowed out with a performance of 'Expresso Bongo' in 1960. It stood on the triangular island formed by Hampshire Terrace, St. Michael's Road and what is now Lord Montgomery Way, a site now occupied by the Polytechnic's Mercantile House.

82. This picture is submitted with a request for further information. Its source simply states it to be a house in Southsea accidentally damaged in the First World War (perhaps 1914) when a shell fired from a British ship bounced off the sea and came inland. Any corroboration or further details of the incident would be welcome.

The Shell King of Southsea

Photo by Oscar Owers, Southsea

83. A well-known local character in the early years of this century was Alfred George Wilkins, pictured here in one of his shell adorned costumes. As well as his personal ornamentation, Mr. Wilkins also decorated his house in Albert Grove, Southsea, with shells and gave lantern slide lectures on his hobby of which he was an acknowledged expert. In the business world, he was a member of a local coach building family which had its premises in St. Edward's Road.

84. This colossal mass of steel and concrete was built at Shoreham in 1917 to serve as a defensive platform in mid-channel, but was not completed in time to make its contribution to the war effort. Intended to be one of six such structures to straddle the channel between Dover and the French Coast, they were to have anti-submarine nets strung between them and were designed to have search-lights and gun batteries which would have been manned by almost one hundred men based on each platform. The tower pictured here was one of only two actually constructed, its companion finally being dismantled. The 'Nab' was sensibly used by Trinity House as a replacement for the Nab Lightship and was towed to, and settled on the shoal, five miles off the Isle of Wight. Whilst not strictly within our city limits, it is certainly included in the environs of Portsmouth and is a feature of our maritime skyline, being 160 feet in height!

85. A railway line from Fratton to Southsea opened on 1st July 1885 and had a precarious existence until the outbreak of the First World War provided the excuse to close it. The original terminus in Granada Road was a grandiose three-platformed affair. Initially services were locomotive hauled, with through carriages to or from London on six of the fifteen trains each day. The line was operated jointly by the London and South Western and London, Brighton and South Coast Railways. The engine seen here in the station was one of the latter's A1 class. Preston was built in 1875 and withdrawn in 1925. Several of the class still survive on various preserved lines. (Photo Lens of Sutton.)

86. The Southsea railway was not a success. It was too short to capture much local traffic, and through passengers found it quicker to start or complete their journey by tram, since reversal or change of trains was necessary at Fratton. In the interests of economy, the big terminus was closed in 1904, the service having been reduced the previous year to a shuttle to Fratton operated every twenty minutes by one of two specially built steam railcars. The much less pretentious wooden shack seen here on the right was built as a replacement. The original buildings became a garage, parts still surviving as such. The station was known as Southsea from 1885 to 1896, and then as East Southsea until closure.

87. The Southsea trains had their own platform at Fratton, located where the carriage washing plant now stands. This is where railcar number 1 is pictured. When they were introduced in June 1903, the engine units had vertical boilers, and an excellent view of number 2 in this condition is contained in Edwin Course's 'Portsmouth Railways' (Portsmouth City Council, 1969). These boilers were not very successful; number 1 had been given the horizontal boiler seen here by October that year, and number 2 got one by June 1904. The carriage part accommodated twelve first-class passengers on plush-covered longitudinal benches and thirty third-class on laterally arranged rush-top seats. (Photo Lens of Sutton.)

88. The Southsea branch passed under Goldsmith Avenue soon after leaving Fratton Station. The signal just beyond the cattle dock remained long after other signalling on the line had been abolished. This view shows tram lines being laid across the bridge circa 1909, and abounds in period detail. The Southsea branch was originally planned to leave the main line at Copnor, and there was once an idea to take another branch off it, follow the line of Goldsmith Avenue and the old canal, cross the entrance of Langstone Harbour on a bridge, and connect with the Hayling Island branch. A circular service would have operated, but the plan never saw fruition. (Photo courtesy of Portsmouth City Records Office.)

89. Here is a scene that few people now living will recognise. This is Devonshire Avenue, looking towards Jessie Road bridge, under which the Southsea Railway passed. The road at right angles to the left is St. Augustine Road. When the railway opened in 1885, there was a level crossing here. By 1904, the replacement bridge had been built beside it, which accounts for the unusual width of Devonshire Square today. A simple platform, known as Jessie Road Bridge Halt, was opened here on 1st October 1904. The line closed in 1914, but the bridge survived until 1926. This view provides incidentally a good idea of the state of the roads in the pre-tarmac era.

90. The third bridge over the Southsea railway was at Albert Road, seen here in about 1925. The Gaiety Cinema across the road had opened in 1924, and the bridge had been levelled by 1926. Albert Road Bridge was the site of the other halt opened in 1904 in a vain attempt to compete with the trams. Old Bridge Buildings in Highland Road are a reminder of the long lost railway. The cinema closed in 1959 and became a supermarket. Old Bridge Road, between St. Ronan's Road and Craneswater Avenue marks the site of the fourth (apparently unphotographed) and last bridge over the line. (Many interesting pictures of railways in the Portsmouth area are in Mitchell and Smith's 'South Coast Railways, Chichester to Portsmouth', Middleton Press, 1984.)

St. James Church, Milton.

91. Until the end of the eighteenth century, the Milton area was largely either jungle or bog, with malaria prevalent in the stagnant water and smugglers in the profusion of more navigable creeks. Tree-felling and drainage improved matters, and a hamlet grew round the junction of what is now Priory Crescent and Milton Road. By 1841, there was sufficient population to warrant the construction of a church. St. James' was consecrated by the Bishop of Winchester on 30th September that year (the same day as Holy Trinity, Portsea), on land presented by Admiral Sir Philip and Lady Henderson Durham.

92. St. James' used to be known as the 'Runaway Church'. One explanation is that eloping couples used to go there to be married because in its early days it was outside the borough boundaries and hence its jurisdiction, but this must be inaccurate because the boundary extensions of 1832 included this area; another is simply that its quiet rural situation was preferred by those couples who wanted to be 'far from the madding crowd'. Originally a daughter church to St. Mary's, Portsea, St. James' gained its own parish in 1844. The church was Norman in style, with pillars in the middle and the circular chancel shown here. Rapid population growth in the area eventually overtook its 200 seat capacity, and on 25th July 1913 the existing church, unusually running north-south, was consecrated and the building illustrated passed into memories.

93. Vicars of St. James' were instrumental in two major civic developments in their parish. Reverend Taylor (vicar from 1894 to 1907) led successful public pressure for provision of tram services along Goldsmith Avenue, and his successor Reverend Fowler (vicar from 1907 to 1916) headed the equally successful local agitation for the preservation of what is now Milton Park as an open space. In 1911, the local landowner 'Jimmy' Goldsmith died, and his farm was to be sold for building development. However, local pressure prevailed, and the land was acquired by the Corporation (along with what is now Bransbury Park) for recreational use. Here is a view of old farm buildings in Milton Park.

94. The first organised religious activities in the Milton area seem to have started sometime in the 1830s, when a Sunday School, in a cottage with one room licensed for worship, was run by members of the Orange Street Congregational Church, and regular services were conducted by the King Street (Portsea) congregation. The chapel illustrated here was built in 1842. A branch of the local Public Library opened on this site in 1925, but Congregational worship continued in what was originally the Kendall memorial chapel, a little further north and on the opposite side of Milton Road. Mr. Kendall was a much-loved pastor of the church illustrated.

95. The commercial hub of the village would have been the post office, seen here on its original site just inside Priory Crescent. Next to it is a grocery/confectionery concern, and then the Brewers Arms, a pub which still survives here in name. The villas to the far right, one of which housed a hardware business, were destroyed in the blitz, and a garage now occupies their site.

The Old Smithy, Milton Portsmouth
J.W.S. 1162

96. Just inside Priory Crescent from its junction with Milton Road, about where the barn of the Milton Arms public house now stands, was a wheelwright's establishment, run latterly by a John Ball. The position of the horse apparently being shod is misleading because a smithy was in fact on the opposite side of the road. Both businesses had disappeared by 1917.

The Old Locks at Milton.

97. Milton lock is the most obvious visible reminder of the Portsmouth Canal, which opened on 19th September 1822 as part of a route via the Arun, the Wey and connecting canals to the Thames and London. It terminated in a basin just about where Allders department store now stands. It could take ships of 150 tons, but although a reasonable amount of traffic came south, return loads were always hard to find. The owners constructed a quay near Portsbridge in 1830, with a cut to give direct access to the harbour, and the canal closed in June 1831. There was one other lock, 200 yards along from that shown. The derelict Milton lock still just survives, but the corresponding view today is not nearly so rural.

98. From its terminus, the canal ran in the cutting now used by the railway as far as Fratton Station, then along the line of what is now Goldsmith Avenue to the White House at Milton, where it turned slightly northwards to reach Langstone Harbour. In the Milton area, there were bridges where Hill Lane (now Winter Road/Priory Crescent) crossed the canal, at the White House and in Ironbridge Lane, where the cottages illustrated here were situated.

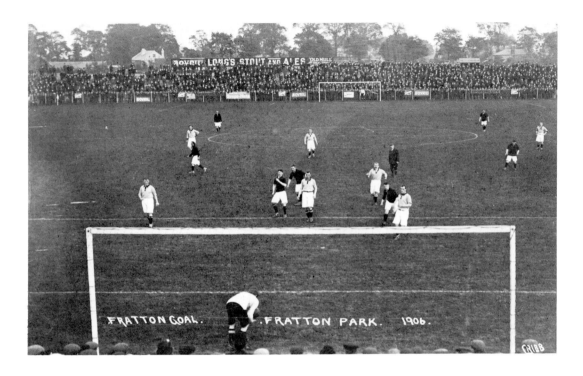

FRATTON GOAL. .FRATTON PARK. 1906. CRIBB

99. In 1898, the founders of the Portsmouth Football and Athletic Company purchased for £7,000 five acres of market garden west of Milton village. This became Fratton Park. For 22 seasons Pompey (as the football team has long been known) played in the Southern League, then in the newly-formed third division south of the Football League until 1924, when they were promoted to division two. They gained first division status in 1927. This postcard is dated 15th September 1906, when Pompey were in the Southern League division one, and played in salmon pink strips. That was a Saturday of a home match (they beat Reading 2-1), so this view is perhaps of the previous home game (1st September) when they beat Plymouth 4-0.

100. On 13th September 1913, Pompey played Coventry City in a Southern League division one match. Here is part of the 12,000 crowd that day who witnessed a scoreless draw. An interesting fashion note is the fact that every man seen wears a hat, whether naval, military or civilian.

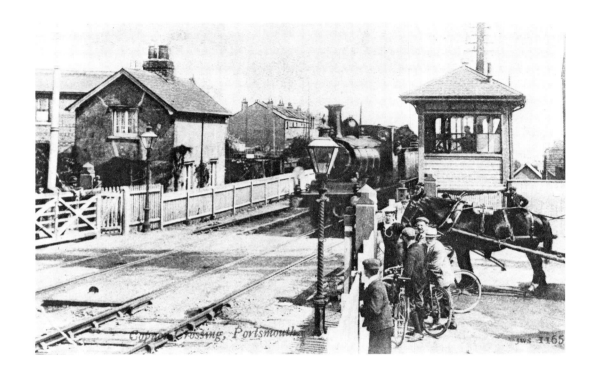

Copnor Crossing, Portsmouth

JWS 1165

101. From the opening of the railway in 1847 until the construction of Copnor Bridge in 1908, vehicular and pedestrian traffic crossed the line at Copnor by means of the level crossing illustrated here. In the 1880s, there was considerable local pressure for a station at this site, and a Station Road, visible in the upper left of this view, was built. Early plans envisaged the Southsea Railway joining the main line at this point. Neither event transpired, Fratton Station being built as the junction instead. The locomotive appears to be one of the C2 class, designed for the London, Brighton and South Coast Railway by R.J. Billinton.

102. This aerial view of 1929 shows part of Copnor. Old farm buildings are seen on the south side of Baffins Pond, which was acquired by the Corporation only in 1934, but perhaps of most interest is the dog track in the centre of the picture. After some rumblings of local opposition, greyhound racing began on 30th June 1928, and meetings were held every Saturday and Wednesday (and eventually Monday as well). A Portsmouth speedway team had a short-lived existence here in the early 1930s. 'Tiger' Hart, Jack Douglas and Bill Clibbett were among its stars. The area eventually became playing fields, and Portsmouth Football Club used it as a training ground for a time. The field still exists at the time of writing, but may soon be built on. (Photo courtesy of Hampshire County Library, Portsmouth.)

Town Hall, Portsmouth.

Parker & Co., Landport

103. A new Town Hall to replace that in High Street was begun in 1886 on or near a site which in the previous century had accommodated Ridge's brewhouse and more recently the official residence of the colonel commanding the Southern District Artillery. On 9th August 1890, the Town Hall was opened by the Prince and Princess of Wales. It became known as the Guildhall in 1926 when Portsmouth attained the status of a city. On 10th January 1941, it was reduced to a shell by enemy bombing, with only the walls and the much damaged tower surviving. The Queen formally opened the rebuilt Guildhall on 8th June 1959. The dome on the tower and minarets on the sides were among several features lost in the rebuilding.

Town Hall from Park, Portsmouth

104. The previous view must date from the very early years of the century as the Technical Institute shown in this view and not present there opened in 1908. Victoria Park, whence this picture is taken, was opened by the Mayor, Mr. William King, on 25th May 1878 on land released by the War Office. In its early days it was sometimes referred to as the People's Park. A bandstand and associated activities were a feature for many years.

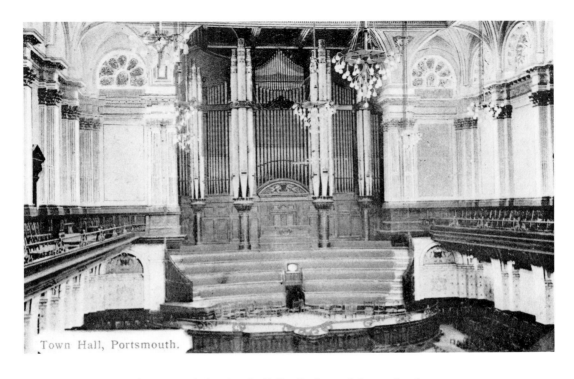

Town Hall, Portsmouth.

105. The Town Hall originally included accommodation for the Police Station and Courts, for the Sanitary Committee and the Tramway Committee, over and above its civic functions. The total cost was £137,098. Here is the Great Hall, 129 feet long, 70 feet wide, and 60 feet high, with seating for 2,000. Municipally-run variety shows on Saturday nights were very popular, at one penny for the floor, two for the gallery. Minstrels shows always drew the biggest audiences. The four-manual organ, one of the largest in the South, was built by Gray and Davidson at a cost of £3,750. The bellows were worked by a 2 horse-power gas engine, and they could also be pumped manually, 16 men being required for this.

Russell Street, Landport.

106. Here is a scene that the combination of Hitler's bombers and post-war redevelopers have rendered unrecognisable. This is Russell Street, immediately to the east of Commercial Road (now Guildhall Walk), south of the Guildhall Square. As a clue to orientation, the statue of Queen Victoria occupies exactly the same spot today. Until 1849 a pond, originally known as Magdalene or Maudlin Pond, later as Ridge's Pond and finally as Tollervey's Pond, was in what became the apex of the junction of Russell Street and Commercial Road. It was filled in with spoil from the newly constructed adjacent railway yard. Russell Street was one of pleasant shops; the few that survived the blitz had all gone by the early 1970s.

MUNICIPAL COLLEGE, PORTSMOUTH.

107. Higher Education had its beginnings in Portsmouth in 1870, with the opening of the Portsmouth and Gosport School of Science and Art. After various changes of name and location, this became Portsmouth Municipal College on the opening of the building illustrated in 1908. It is still in use, but whereas then it also housed the College of Art, the Central Public Library, and a Teachers' Training College, it now accommodates part of just two of the 21 departments of Portsmouth Polytechnic. The chimney in the background belonged to the old swimming baths, replaced by those in Anglesea Road in 1963. Until January 1970, Park Road ran right through to St. George's Road. This end of it is now called King Henry I Street.

Opening of Portsmouth Municipal College.

108. The College, built behind the Town Hall on a plot of land known as Mayor's Lawn, was officially opened by the Lord Mayor, Councillor F.G. Foster, on 10th September 1908. This was preceded by a reception in the Town Hall given by the Mayoress, his six year old daughter, Doris. There was then a procession, seen here, down the Town Hall steps and round the corner to the College, in this order: College staff, Corporation officials, the Mayor, Corporation and Education Committee, various teachers and visitors. The 'Evening News' of 11th September lists many of those present; it also prognosticated 'The work... done at the College will not be merely of local, but national importance', a prophecy amply born out today by the College's direct descendant, Portsmouth Polytechnic.

109. In 1865, the Reverend Reginald Shutte, curate of Holy Trinity, established a mission church in White's Row, one of the most brothel-ridden streets in Portsea. As a result of his efforts and the support of the author, the Reverend Charles Kingsley, White's Row was eventually demolished and a new church to serve the area founded. Dedicated to St. Michael and All Angels, it stood at the junction of Park Road and St. Michael's Road. Work begin in 1872, but, because of local opposition to Shutte's ritualism, it was not ready for consecration until 1882, and, even then, only the nave and aisles were built.

St. Michaels, Portsmouth.

110. St. Michael's was designed by William Butterfield. By 1892, funds had become available for its completion. Mr. Hubbuck describes it as 'one of the great Anglo-Catholic churches of Portsea'. It sustained slight bomb damage in 1941, but was able to take on the rôle of Chapel to the Royal Naval Barracks after the virtual destruction of Holy Trinity the same year. Some consideration was given to its secular use by the then College of Technology before it was demolished in 1960. The Polytechnic has commemorated the church by naming its Science Services block, which stands on the site, 'St. Michael's Building'.

16 PORTSMOUTH. — *Royal Seamen and Marines' Orphans Schools.* — L.L.

111. There is evidence of a chapel dating from the fourteenth century, dedicated to Mary Magdalene, serving as a leper hospital and general hostelry for pilgrims and travellers, near the eastern end of what is now St. Michael's Road. Run by priors, it was destroyed at the Reformation. It is coincidental that, centuries later, various establishments for the help of others were built near the site. The (still standing) offices of the Board of Guardians date from 1879. Next to them, illustrated here, was the Seamen and Marines' Orphan Home, which had moved to St. Michael's Road in 1876 from Lion Terrace, having been in St. George's Square 1834-1851. Beyond the orphanage, St. Andrew's Presbyterian Church (1880-1982) can be glimpsed.

112. The Hippodrome Theatre, seen on the right of this view, was yet another important building destroyed in the blitz of 10th-11th January 1941. It stood on the corner of Commercial Road (now Guildhall Walk) and Salem Street (now Dorothy Dymond Street), almost opposite the Theatre Royal. It operated mostly as a music hall, but an occasional play, circus or pantomime was staged. The site of the old Hippodrome remained Portsmouth's longest surviving bomb-site, redevelopment starting only in 1984. By coincidence, it provided what is to be hoped will be Portsmouth's last unexploded bomb of the Second World War, when a 500 pound monster was unearthed on 12th October, and made safe the following day.

MISS MARIE TEMPEST LAYING
COMMEMORATION STONE
17TH MAY. HIPPODROME
FLASHLIGHT PHOTO: PORTSMOUTH
RECE SILK TOPIC

113. The Hippodrome was originally owned by Sir Walter de Frece, husband of Vesta Tilley. The formal opening in May 1907 was performed by one of the leading comédiennes of the day, Miss Marie Tempest (1864-1942). Afterwards, the invited audience of 1,000 (including Vesta Tilley) watched a typical music-hall show that included a bioscope, common in variety theatres of the time.

Commercial Road, Portsmouth

114. This southern part of Commercial Road up as far as Edinburgh Road was known as Landport Road until the 1890s. The building on the left was the General Post Office, opened on 10th June 1883. (Before then, the main post office was in High Street, and, pre-1858, in what is now Pembroke Road.) This one was in turn replaced by a new edifice in Slindon Street in 1976, and demolished. Across the road is the forecourt of what is always known locally as the Town Station, although its official names have been as follows: Portsmouth, 1847-1861; Portsmouth and Southsea, 1861-1876; Portsmouth Town, 1876-1921; Portsmouth and Southsea, 1921 to date.

33 *PORTSMOUTH. — Commercial Road. —*

115. A little further north from the previous view, this shows the junctions with Edinburgh Road on the left, and Arundel Street, further up on the right. The Landport Drapery Bazaar, a well-known store for many years, is on the corner. Its site is the terminus of the Portsmouth to Arundel Canal (see picture 97), whence the name Arundel Street. The street market used to be held in Commercial Road, but subsequently moved to Charlotte Street. Until the 1890s, the part of what is now Commercial Road from Edinburgh Road to Lake Road was known as Union Road, commemorating the union of Portsmouth and Portsea for administering the Poor Law.

Empire Palace, Edinburgh Road,   *Landport.*

116. After the demolition of the fortifications in the 1870s, what had been Lion Gate Road was straightened out and renamed Edinburgh Road. Prominent in this view, on the left, is the Empire Music Hall. This opened in 1891, and it had a particularly fine promenade where one could get a drink while watching the show. In 1913, Marie Lloyd was the star turn when the refurbished hall re-opened as the Coliseum. The name reverted to the Empire in 1950, and the hall lasted until 1958 when it was demolished and replaced by a supermarket.

Catholic Cathedral

J. R. Penning, Fine Art Dealer, 10 Elm Grove, Southsea.   &211ª222

117. After some debate on the relative merits of Southampton or Portsmouth for the see town of a new diocese to cover the Channel Islands, the Isle of Wight, Berkshire and Hampshire, the Roman Catholic authorities eventually decided on the latter, and what was originally to be just a parish church became the cathedral. Work started in 1880 with J. Crawley as architect. He died a year later, and until 1892 J. Hansom (son of the inventor of Hansom cabs) was in charge. Crawley planned a spire 200 feet high, which would have made it the tallest building in Portsmouth. This never materialised. The building was finished under the aegis of Canon A. Scoles. The two turrets he added at the west end in 1906 are not present in this view.

118. The interior of the cathedral has undergone two major changes in its lifetime. Originally, the sanctuary was largely cut off from the congregation by a wrought iron screen across the chancel arch. In 1906 the high altar was moved forward to the centre of the chancel, and the screen put behind it. Then in 1971, after much discussion the previous year, more alterations took place to accommodate the latest liturgical practices. Together with substantial redecoration, they revealed much more of the cathedral's beauty. The baldacchino over the altar on its columns of red Peterhead marble shown here was removed at this time.

COMMERCIAL ROAD, PORTSMOUTH.

119. It is not easy to imagine that before the war there were no less than five turnings eastwards off Commercial Road between Arundel Street and Lake Road. On the north corner of the first of these, Chandos Street, the large building with the turret was the Royal Sailors' Rest, run by Dames Agnes Weston and Sophia Wintz. This was immensely popular with the 'blue-jackets', providing a 'cabin' and a meal for any for whom there was room. Temperance and religious activities were provided, but were in no way compulsory. In her autobiography, Agnes Weston gives the date of opening as 13th June 1881. The Rest was destroyed in the blitz of 10th January 1941, but its work continued afterwards at various locations.

120. Agnes Weston perhaps belongs as much to Devonport as to Portsmouth, but she did so much good for so many people in our town that the inclusion of a portrait of her is easily justified. With her lifelong friend Sophia Wintz she ran the Royal Sailors' Rest at Devonport and Portsmouth until her death in 1918 at the age of 78, and did incalculable good works for sailors and their wives. In developing the Rests, she was able to purchase a number of pubs, which gave her particular pleasure. When this 'Mother of the Navy' died, she was accorded the unprecedented distinction of a funeral with full naval honours.

121. The Rests were often referred to simply as 'Aggie Weston's', so it is often overlooked that they were run jointly with Sophia Wintz, pictured here. The daughter of a wealthy Swiss gentleman, she and Agnes Weston first met in 1873, although they had been at the same study group in Bath the previous year without actually meeting. They worked together until the latter's death in 1918. Miss Wintz was made a Dame of the British Empire in 1921, and died in 1929, when she too was accorded a funeral with full naval honours.

122. A nostalgic reminder of an old-fashioned department store and its prices is given here. B.A. Gale operated this establishment at 175 Commercial Road (near the junction with Meadow Street) from about 1908 to 1916. Valuing was scrupulous and, if any item was worth less than one penny, additional goods such as a few pins were added to the purchase to bring it up to the full amount. Marks and Spencers operated near the site contemporaneously and gradually took over neighbouring premises to finally engulf the Penny Bazaar itself.

123. This last look at Commercial Road provides a wealth of 1930s detail. The tram is on the 16 service, heading for Copnor down Lake Road. The bus, the cars and the cycles (the one on the on-side of the Vauxhall conveying a police sergeant) are all typical of the time. There is still a British Home Stores at this location, but Parker's, David Greig's and McIlroys are businesses here no more.

124. The building shown here, on the corner of Lake Road and Leonard Road, ended its days in the cause of highway development in 1980. Its last commercial use was as a warehouse for a local draper, but for many years it served a very unusual function, as a temperance music hall. It was built by Frank Pearce, a staunch temperance worker, and his brother Bob, in six months in 1884. It was initially let to one Henry Vento, a ventriloquist who ran it as Vento's Music Hall, until 1891. Frank Pearce himself operated it with his wife and two daughters as the People's Palace of Varieties from then until his retirement in 1920. It subsequently became Jury's Picture House and later the Palladium Cinema.

125. Frank Pearce was one of Portsmouth's characters around the turn of the century. His concept of a music hall without prodigious supplies of drink and women was jeered at, yet his People's Palace was a success, and, indeed, he ran a similar hall, the St. James' Palace, in Charlotte Street along similar lines from 1899 to 1920. He was also a keen proponent of vegetarianism, anti-vivisection, phrenology, and, latterly, spiritualism. He served on the Council from 1908 to 1911, was an active Freemason, and also found time to write poetry and edit a magazine. The tombstone he designed for his wife's grave in Milton Cemetery after her death in 1912 was so unusual that it attracted press notices! Frank Pearce died in 1921, and is also buried there.

126. Running almost due north from Charlotte Street was Chance Street, one of a proliferation of low narrow streets to spring up in the early nineteenth century. The area abounded in pubs and brothels, and in 1882 Winchester College established St. Agatha's mission, at first in Charlotte Street. Appointed missioner in 1885 was Reverend Robert Dolling, who summed up his patch as one 'leavened with a low moral tone'. Chance Street accommodated his parsonage for a time, and also an associated mission hall and almshouses. The area did improve over the years, but it was still scheduled for redevelopment when early in 1941 one of the largest explosions of the war flattened the whole district. (Photo courtesy of Point Collectors' Centre.)

127. Father Dolling combined an intense missionary zeal with ultra high churchmanship. (He claimed that the smell of incense disguised the less pleasant odours his flock was used to.) He worked tirelessly for, in the title of his own book, 'Ten years in a Portsmouth Slum', raising all the money to replace his humble mission church with the albeit truncated St. Agatha's still standing. His house was open to all, and he was a fearless battler against the drink problem. After one typical fulmination, the Mayor retorted that he recently visited 50 pubs in 80 minutes and saw no excesses. Dolling's unanswerable response was to ask where else could one possibly visit so many in so short a time? He left in 1896 after a liturgical dispute with his new bishop.

128. Portsmouth is no stranger to Royal visits and it was particularly fitting that the first person to be granted the freedom of the new City, on 23rd July 1926, was H.R.H. the Prince of Wales (later King Edward VIII). After a full day of engagements, he arrived at Fratton Station just after four o'clock, to be seen off to London by a guard of honour composed of the two local divisions of the Voluntary Aid Detachment of the British Red Cross Society and of Portsmouth Girl Guides, Brownies and Rangers, one of each from every unit in the city, under the command of Lady Helen Newcombe, County Commissioner for Hampshire. Note the roof on the station footbridge, removed about 1965.

129. The name Fratton derives from Froddington, one of the manors mentioned in the Domesday Book. The lands of the manor seem to have occupied a good deal of the south central part of Portsea Island, and Fratton Road, shown on some of the earliest maps of the town, would have been the principal means of communication on the estate. In the early years of this century, having grown into a substantial commercial centre, it was still very narrow, and, with the growth of vehicular traffic, extremely dangerous. The narrowness is exemplified here by the interlacing of the tram lines.

130. Alderman J.W. Perkins had been agitating for many years to have Fratton Road widened, and his efforts saw fruition in 1929 when all the buildings on the east side between Fratton Bridge and St. Mary's Church were moved back. The road was properly surfaced, and a double line of tramway track installed. On 22nd July, the Lord Mayor, Councillor J.E. Smith, opened the widened road. The associated celebrations included a procession, and the vehicle illustrated, an old fire-engine, was one of the participants.

St Marys Church Kingston Portsmouth 1843 18.
with old original Tower

131. St. Mary's, Portsea, is the oldest ecclesiastical foundation in Portsmouth, dating from about 1164. It was built by the de Portsea family, owners of much land in the area, roughly equidistant from the villages of Fratton, Copnor and Kingston. The church illustrated was built in 1843 to the design of Thomas Ellis Owen who developed much of Southsea. For some reason it retained the tower of the original mediaeval church. The mass of tombstones clearly tell why St. Mary's Road used to be known as Dead Man's Lane. The third and present St. Mary's was built in 1887. W.H. Smith, the bookseller, Member of Parliament and First Lord of the Admiralty guyed in the Portsmouth-based Gilbert and Sullivan opera 'H.M.S. Pinafore', provided most of the funds.

S 5047　　　BIRDS EYE VIEW OF PO TSMOUTH FROM ST MARYS CHURCH TOWER.

132. St. Mary's has for long been one of the most populous Anglican parishes in the country. The experience of running its several mission churches and organising a staff of, at one time, as many as 17 curates provided ideal training for several of its incumbents to go on to very high office in the Church. (Cosmo Gordon Lang, vicar from 1896 to 1901, was Archbishop of York 1909-1928 and of Canterbury 1929-1942, and Cyril Garbett, vicar from 1909-1919, was Archbishop of York 1942-1955.) This view, looking westwards from the tower of the present church, shows a network of streets of small terraced houses so typical of Portsmouth, especially before the war.

133. On 7th June 1906, two ships of His Imperial Japanese Majesty's Navy, the Katori and the Kashima, visited Portsmouth. That morning, before a civic lunch with the Lord Mayor and a visit to the Theatre Royal, 100 men from each ship were taken on a tour of the town by tram. One of the six vehicles involved is seen here at the junction of Kingston Crescent, London Road and Kingston Road. Behind the tram, the large building (which survives in commercial use) at the time housed a police station and public library. They moved to their new quarters in Kingston Crescent and Gladys Avenue respectively in 1963.

London Road, Portsmouth in 1906. 1160

134. Here is a 1906 view of London Road looking southwards, a little to the north of the junction with Chichester Road. The smithy was already up for sale under the agency of Bott's, next door, at number 34. The estate agency itself was gone by 1912, and all the houses shown here have long since been turned into or rebuilt as various commercial establishments.

London Road & **Gladys Avenue**, Portsmouth.

135. The North End area started off as a purely residential district away from the bustle of Portsmouth and Portsea, but it was soon overtaken by commercial developments. The Poplars, the house in the centre of this view, was the home of Mr. A.W. White, businessman and general manager of the Portsmouth Street Tramways Company for many years. In 1883, in recognition for his having spent a good deal of his own money improving the area, the Council allowed him to name a road. Gladys Avenue, the left branch of the fork, was named after his daughter who was born that year. Gladys White had a very eventful life, written up in 'Hampshire', January 1980.

ST. MARKS CHURCH

136. A short-lived mission had operated from the North End Hall in 1868, and a permanent church dedicated to St. Mark, serving the rapidly increasing population of the area, opened on 8th February 1874, on the corner of Derby Road and London Road. Various additions and alterations occurred over the years. There was talk in the 1920s of making it the cathedral. By the 1960s it became clear that the cost of maintaining the existing fabric would be prohibitive, and the parish council took the bold decision to build a completely new church on the other side of Derby Road. The new building was consecrated in October 1970.

Interior of St. Mark's Church, Portsmouth.

137. The traditional interior of the old St. Mark's provides a vivid contrast with that of the new. There was little particularly remarkable about it, but it was much loved by its parishioners. Final demolition came in March 1971, after moves to preserve the tower and clock on the unlikely pretext, as Mr. L. Bern records, that they had been designed by Brunel.

138. Sir Ernest Shackleton's ship calls at Portsmouth's Flat-house Quay on route for Antarctica in 1921. Local folk flocked to see The Quest which was soon to leave for South Georgia. Shackleton, hero of two previous Antarctic Expeditions died of a heart attack on this, his last adventure, on 5th January 1922, and was buried on a mountain top in the land which he had set out to conquer.

139. Photographed from the air in 1921 is Hilsea Barracks. The site had had a military presence since at least 1756 including a period during the Second World War when the U.S. Army occupied both the Barracks and nearby Rugby Camp. The area today is largely a modern housing estate, Gatcombe Park, thus continuing the association which commenced in 1291 when the 20 or so acres was called Little Gatcombe. The Barracks has, in its day, included a church, military hospital and burial ground and is believed to be the site of an ancient priory.

THE HILSEA LAGOON BOATING POOLS, PORTSMOUTH

M.&Co.   707.

Looking west over the Lagoon which was originally a moat and part of Portsmouth defences built in 1862.
In the far distance is the Keep of Porchester Castle, first built by the Romans.

140. By 1861, the northernmost extremity of Portsea Island had been fortified with a rampart and moat almost all the way across. These had long since ceased to be of any military value when the westernmost section was acquired by the Corporation in 1930. Together with a not very tidy piece of associated foreshore, this had become Hilsea Lido by 1935. This view showing part of the old moat converted into a boating lake differs from the current scene in two respects; the wooden footbridge has yet to appear, and the children's paddle boats are now things of the past. A planned ice-rink at the Lido may soon change the scene more radically.

141. The Hilsea Lines took on their final form in 1861. The London Road passed through the arches illustrated here. The arches became an ever-increasing encumbrance to traffic, and, as a means of finding employment for men returning from the First World War, they were demolished about 1920. Originally built for military purposes, the shed on the right housed the local fire engine in the later years of the Lines' existence.

142. High Street, Cosham in Edwardian years was truly the commercial road of the village, housing as it did almost all of the local business premises. Busy centres such as this always had an abundance of public houses and Cosham's High Street was no exception. Among the several licensed houses which no longer exist was The King and Queen, so obviously named after King Edward VII and his Queen Alexandra. The roof lines would seem to indicate a building of considerable age, probably pre-dating their majesties by several centuries. The premises also contained a small brewery, but nothing now remains of the business and the site has long been re-developed and now houses both an optician's and jeweller's establishments.

143. Volume 3 of the Victoria County History of Hampshire, published in 1908, states that the industries of East Cosham comprised sieve and basket making. Here is a view of Fullick's basket shop, in what is now Havant Road, near its junction with Cosham High Street, in the early years of this century. A local tradition has it that among their products were basket-ware coffins! Any definitive substantiation of this would be most welcome. Fullick's was operational by 1840, and the business lasted until the 1930s. One of the clan, Edward Fullick, was, in 1911, captain of the local volunteer fire brigade.

Drayton, near Cosham.

144. Apart from a few dwellings in what is now Lower Drayton Lane, most of the development of the erstwhile hamlet of Drayton took place in the first quarter of this century, as it blossomed rapidly to become a suburb of Portsmouth. The borough boundary was extended to the top of Portsdown Hill and as far east as Drayton Lane in 1920, but it was not until 1932 that the (now city) boundary was extended to take in the rest of Drayton and Farlington. This view from the early years of this century shows the junction of the Havant Road with Lower Drayton Lane, still very much a rural backwater.

145. This is the palatial grandstand of Portsmouth Park race course which in its day was as prestigious as any in the country. The opening meeting was on 27th June 1891, and, although 'Country Life' of 15th April 1899 states that the course was then up for sale, racing continued until 17th April 1915, when ironically the big race was won by 'Final Shot' (10-1). The War Office took over the site and it became one of the biggest ammunition dumps in Britain. The race course owners tried unsuccessfully to get the site back after the war, and it was eventually sold to the Corporation. Farlington playing fields occupy the site today, and the bridge carrying the Eastern Road over the railway is very close to where the grandstand stood.

THE MILITARY HOSPITAL, PORTSDOWN HILL

146. Queen Alexandra Hospital had a somewhat paradoxical start to life, being a military hospital built by the Navy! There was an earlier military hospital in Lion Terrace, built on land made available by the demolition of the fortifications. The Admiralty took this over around 1900, and built the Queen Alexandra as a replacement. From 1926, it was used solely for accommodating persons disabled in the First World War. It took in its first civilian patients in 1941, after bomb damage to the Royal Hospital in Commercial Road. The hospital was much expanded in the 1970s, and when in 1979 the Royal closed the Queen Alexandra assumed most of its functions.

147. A church has existed at Wymering since the twelfth century. The lych gate, giving access to the cemetery across the road, could not claim that degree of antiquity, but it had been a local landmark for many years when, because of its rotten and consequently dangerous condition, it had to be demolished in August 1950. An appeal to raise £107 to restore it realised just £1, and supervising the demolition was one of the last duties of the then vicar, the Reverend E.W. Babbage, before he retired.

148. Our picture shows racing in Paulsgrove in 1929 at Wymering Park. This course, like its early predecessor at Farlington was closed at the start of a World War and was not re-opened. The winning jockey in this photograph is Mr. Sydney Hall who now farms in Herefordshire. The horse's name was Abbaye de la Paix.

149. Another photograph of Wymering Park shows the Paddock and Restaurant area. Later, Wymering was to be linked with another course at Northolt and both were to stage pony racing. The paddock shown here covers an area which to-day is Marsden Road, Paulsgrove. Like the Farlington course of earlier years, Wymering Park had access to the main line railway with its own local platform.

150. Horse bus operations in Portsmouth seem to have started in 1840, with a service from Southsea to North End via Old Portsmouth and the Hard. By the 1880s, the Provincial Tramways Company had at least three 'single-horse' bus services. One is known to have operated from the Dockyard Main Gate to the end of Edinburgh Road. The vehicle illustrated here, with the dockyard wall behind it, was probably waiting to work this route. (Photo courtesy of Portsmouth City Records Office.)

151. The Landport and Southsea Company provided the first tram service in Portsmouth, opening in 1865 between the Town Station and Clarence Pier, which was enlarged to allow the cars to run on to its deck. The Provincial Tramways Company opened its first route from the Floating Bridge to North End in 1874, and a Kingston, Fratton, Buckland and Southsea Tramways Company began operating in 1883. In 1901, all the services were municipalised. Electrification began that year, and the last horse tram ran in Cosham in 1903. The horse-tram shown here is at the Esplanade Hotel. The lack of an owner's name on the side suggests a date of 1878, when the Landport Company sold out to Provincial; the old name had been painted out, the new was yet to appear.

152. This is Corporation tram number 62, going westwards along Western Parade. 62 was one of the batch of eighty built for the inaugural municipalised routes by Dick Kerr and Company Limited from 1900 to 1902. These vehicles had two 25 horse power motors, and 55 seats. Note the low position of the headlight; Corporation trams could always be distinguished from those of the Horndean Company (see next page) in the dark as the latter had their headlights set much higher. Tram services in Portsmouth came to an end on 10th November 1936.

S 10850   LIGHT RLY. TERMINUS, COSHAM.

153. The Portsdown and Horndean Light Railway operated trams between Cosham and Horndean from 2nd March 1903 until 9th January 1935. For the last few years, it had running powers over the Corporation's tracks to Portsmouth and Southsea. The emerald green and cream cars were very popular in their hey-day, and there were (never fulfilled) schemes to extend the system to Denmead and Petersfield. The effects of road competition were already being felt when the abandonment of some of the Corporation's tramways deprived the Horndean Company of access into the city and effectively ended its viability. The company sold out to Southdown Motor Services. This view shows Horndean car number 4 at the terminus in Cosham.

CLARENCE PIER TERMINUS

154. In October and November 1920, 12 new trams for the Corporation services, numbered 105-116, were delivered by English Electric. They were the first Portsmouth cars to have totally enclosed bodies, and, apart from one experimental vehicle introduced in 1930, they were the last trams built for Portsmouth. This picture of 116 also provides a good view of the front of Clarence Pier and the Esplanade Hotel. The location is the same as that of the horse tram shown on picture 151.

155. In 1933, the Council decided to replace their trams with trolley buses, and the first such vehicles appeared the following year. The first few were a miscellaneous collection, but, in 1936-37, 76 Craven bodied AEC 52 seaters came into use. Number 273, seen here at the Canoe Lake, was introduced on 14th November 1936. It ran until 3rd December 1961, and it was scrapped the following year by Messrs. Strudwick at Bedhampton chalk pit. (Photo courtesy of Peter Relf.)

156. The last batch of trolley buses were 15 Burlingham vehicles on British United Traction chassis with English Electric equipment, introduced in 1950-51. They also had 52 seats. Numbered 301-315, all but number 303 lasted until the final month of trolley bus services in July 1963. Number 313 (introduced 1st March 1951) is seen here in Greetham Street. It had the doleful distinction of operating the final service on 27th July. This class were usually to be found on the 5/6 and 15/16 routes, so this view of 313 on an 18 service is comparatively unusual. 313 was preserved. (Photo courtesy of Peter Relf.)